THE
QUALITY
POCKETBOOK

By Anthony Mitchell

Drawings by Alan Roe

". . . Excellent, distils the enormous body of writing and thinking that exists in this area
into a very readable, surprisingly complete and authoritative introduction and overview.
I would recommend this book to anyone who feels instinctively that a total quality
programme is essential, but has not had the time, or the resources, to find out why."
Peter Leathley, Employee Relations Director, Sittingbourne Paper Company

"An essential guide for the manager looking to ensure that the company is at the
forefront in the 21st Century."
Caroline Black, Divisional Director, Kelvin UK

Published by:
Management Pocketbooks Ltd
14 East Street, Alresford, Hants SO24 9EE, U.K.
Tel: +44 (0)1962 735573   Fax: +44 (0)1962 733637
E-mail: pocketbks@aol.com
http://members.aol.com/pocketbks

First Published 1994. Reprinted 1997, 1999.

© Anthony Mitchell 1994

ISBN: 1 870471 21 0

British Library Cataloguing-in-Publication Data – A catalogue record for this book
is available from the British Library.

Printed in U.K. by: Alresford Press Ltd, Prospect Road, Alresford, Hants

CONTENTS

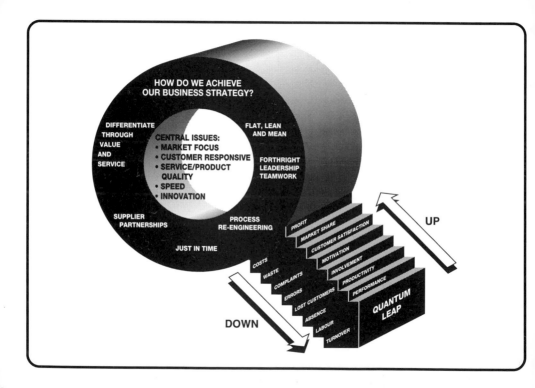

WHAT IS QUALITY?

DEFINE YOUR TERMS

Quality means different things to different people.

Quality is confused with luxury, eg:

- an expensive car
- designer label clothes
- gold plated lighter

BUT.... if YOU (the customer) wish to:

move garden refuse	—	an expensive car may not suit your purpose
decorate the house	—	designer clothes would be inappropriate
give up smoking	—	a gold lighter would be of little value

WHAT IS QUALITY?

QUALITY NOT LUXURY

When the phrase Total Quality Management (TQM) is used we do NOT mean luxury, but rather such concepts as:

- **does the product meet my requirements?**
- **is it suitable, or fit for my purpose?**
- **will the service delight me?**
- **is the service, or product, of value? (a function of both quality and price).**

To add to the confusion, and unfortunate jargon, some organisations choose NOT to call their initiative TQM preferring just TQ or QM !! It may be a benefit not to label part of your strategy in this way — TQM should not become another 'flavour of the month'.

WHAT IS QUALITY?

HAS THE MEANING CHANGED?

Yes, for many people and organisations.

Quality Control

- Places emphasis on inspection and checking.
- Take out the scrap.
- The role of the inspector is to check the work of others.

    Focus: The **amount** of work

Quality Assurance

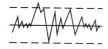

- Work to systems and procedures.
- Design quality in where possible and follow a particular method.
- This helps consistency and conformance.

    Focus: The **way** work is done

4

HAS THE MEANING CHANGED?

Quality Management

- Everyone is responsible for the quality of their own work, ie: check own work before passing the work on.
- This implies doing the right thing, and doing it right first time.
- (PS The customer sets the standard.)

Customer supply chain

Focus: The **results** of what is done.

WHAT IS QUALITY?

WHAT IS TOTAL QUALITY (MANAGEMENT)?
BE SPECIFIC

Take care! The more some get involved with Quality, so it begins to take on an all embracing, rather nebulous definition. This can be very frustrating for others who seek a more specific view.

It may help to refine one of the popular definitions to suit your own industry or circumstances. Some companies have a 'Quality Policy' as a statement of their values with regard to customers, employees and suppliers, etc.

The late Dr W Edwards Deming said:

'Good quality does not necessarily mean high quality. It means a predictable degree of uniformity and dependability with a quality suited to the market.'

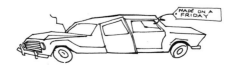

WHAT IS TOTAL QUALITY (MANAGEMENT)?

DEFINITIONS

Others have broken down the definition of TQM as:

QUALITY **Continually satisfying requirements.**
(In some industries it is important to **delight** the customer, ie: satisfy the need, but also add value (eg: excellent after sales service) at little to no extra cost. This needs to be balanced; in other businesses where there is a tendency to over engineer, the customer may not be prepared to pay!

TOTAL QUALITY **Continuously improving customer satisfaction levels <u>and</u> simultaneously improving margins.**

TOTAL QUALITY MANAGEMENT **Achieving total quality through gaining everyone's commitment and involvement.**

QUALITY — COMMON SENSE?

For many, the principles are just common sense — if it were your own business, that's how you would operate. Whilst TQM is different from how we used to regard just Quality, it is not necessarily new — often just undoing the bad habits from years of:

- 'make 'em cheap and pile 'em high'

- poor management — them & us, a lack of clear leadership

- measurement systems which rewarded the wrong behaviour and so on

Regrettably this is easy to say but hard to do!

QUALITY — COMMON SENSE?

TQM IS

- Customers set standards
- Reduction of total costs
- Continuous improvement

- Management leading strategic change of which quality is a part, throughout the organisation

- Avoiding waste by eliminating errors
- Doing the right things to add value
- Using everyone

TQM IS NOT

- Solely meeting own standards
- Compromising quality - on the cheap
- Control

- Quality experts checking product specification

- Luxury

ARE YOU A 'QUALITY' MANAGER?

TQM requires that <u>you</u> demonstrate what you say, both to gain commitment and <u>earn</u> respect.

This will mean striving for a balance, to meet the differing needs and to resolve the possible tensions that emerge between:

Individuals

- Who may have different learning styles. The 'Quality' Manager makes use of coaching and facilitating where appropriate. Encourage individuals and the organisation to learn from mistakes!

Groups

- Some may progress to 'self managed' status.
- Collaboration across groups and with other parts of the company may increasingly be required.

ARE YOU A 'QUALITY' MANAGER?

Results

- Individuals increasingly have a say in 'what to do and how to do it'.
- The manager needs to ensure that desired results are achieved and meet overall business goals.

Change

- Learn to LOVE change (it won't go away).
- Change will be continuous, sometimes radical, at other times evolutionary.
- TQM requires continuous improvement.

WHAT IS QUALITY?

WHY IS TQM IMPORTANT?

The last ten years or so have seen a Quality revolution take place initially in the US then more recently throughout Europe. **WHY?**

There are a number of pressures, including:

- **JAPAN**   Japanese companies dominate world trade in a number of markets, especially manufacturing of electronic products, but also in key services, eg: Banking (ranked by asset value). In Japan there is a firm belief in getting the best out of all employees and in attention to detail.

- **CUSTOMERS** Have become much more demanding. Travel has helped to change expectations, as have changes in trade barriers. Complaints are seen as an opportunity to improve. Value is an increasingly important consideration as customers struggle to balance the **relative** price and quality levels offered between suppliers.

WHY IS TQM IMPORTANT?

- **SUPPLIERS**   Are under greater pressure than ever before. Companies are looking to reduce their supply base to improve consistency, reduce costs and seek partnership with the vital few. (In times of industrial relations conflict the opposite approach, spreading the risk, is more common)
  The bureaucracy of Quality has led to greater power in the hands of purchasers — often imposing systems (BS 5750/ISO 9000) on those competing for business.

- **EMPLOYEES**   For years the shop floor have argued that it was management that had it wrong!
  Through greater involvement, teamwork and responsibility employees become not only more motivated but also more productive and effective.
  Nobody wishes to·be associated with lousy quality!

DOES TQM GIVE COMPETITIVE ADVANTAGE?

- If you are first (with the implementation of TQM) in your industry, or market segment then **YES.**

- In industries where the competition are fighting over **price,** then differentiation through **quality,** coupled with careful positioning and pricing, may make the vital difference, eg: Club Med (travel), Milliken (textiles), etc.

- Again where cost competition is fierce, TQM can be a long term initiative for **both** raising quality and reducing costs through eliminating:
    - waste   - rework   - unnecessary checking, etc;

  and
    - adding value to those dimensions which are important to the customer.

As image and perceptions change, you may then be able to move upmarket as quality increases, to market segments where higher margins may be achieved. Japanese car makers such as Toyota are a good example.

IS TQM NECESSARY TO STAY IN THE RACE?

Probably **YES.** For many TQM is now a necessary (but not sufficient) condition.

- In a number of markets, eg: computers, chemicals, fast food, appropriate levels of quality only qualify the companies to compete, ie: it becomes an entry condition. They still have to win business based upon price, delivery or reliability, etc.

- As a result of continuous improvement the goal posts keep shifting. Getting **better at being better** is the challenge.

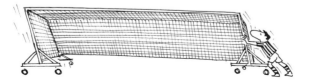

WHAT IS QUALITY?

KEY QUESTIONS

For those just starting
- What does Quality (or a lack of it) mean for your business — to customers/ suppliers/employees/shareholders?
- If there is pressure to improve quality, where is it coming from and why?
- Do your competitors have Quality Improvement initiatives? If so, can you afford NOT to have a TQM process — and what can you do to make it different?

For those who already have a TQM initiative
- What were the reasons for starting, and have they now changed?
- Have you made progress in improving attitudes/expectations of customers/ suppliers/employees. If not, what are the main barriers, and what needs to be done to achieve a breakthrough?
- Is TQM part of your business strategy?
  If so, are costs being reduced in key areas and are service/response times improving as planned?
  If not, what can be done to prevent TQM being regarded as a separate activity — more involvement of senior management, more interdepartmental activity, closer working with suppliers, etc?
- Have internal customer supply chains been identified and agreed?

QUALITY AND PROFIT

QUALITY AND PROFIT

ARE THEY LINKED?

YES there is a positive link.

There is evidence that high performing organisations enjoy both financial success and high ratings of customer satisfaction. This has been verified by consultancy surveys, benchmarking exercises and increasingly popular forms of self assessment.

In recent years a number of lessons have led to improved profit and quality.

- Do not focus on internal improvements without also paying attention to the marketplace, competition and external factors: *see section 4.*

- Do measure improvements in performance/cost reduction and ensure that systems are in place both to implement the benefits and to track the results: *see sections 5/6.*

- Do tackle issues which are business related and incorporated in the business plan. Not just superficial exercises which get people involved but result in little lasting benefit or change.

QUALITY AND PROFIT

A NOTE OF CAUTION

****
HEALTH WARNING!
****

TQM is **NOT** a panacea for success. Companies with successful track records, sophisticated TQM and process management skills may still decline in profitability for a number of reasons, eg:

- incorrect product strategy
- poor distribution channels
- weak leadership.

Under such circumstances a decline in performance may be in spite of TQM rather than because of it.

WILL IMPROVED QUALITY COST MORE?
LONG TERM VIEW

It has been said that 'Quality is Free' (Philip Crosby).
The implication being that quality improvements arise from:

- waste reduction
- eliminating rework
- eliminating non value-added activities.

Hence in the long term quality should
not cost the organisation more.

QUALITY AND PROFIT

WILL IMPROVED QUALITY COST MORE?
SHORT TERM VIEW

In the short term it rather depends on where you are starting from!
Additional costs to budget for might include:

- consultancy fees
- training materials, workshops
- system improvements, BS 5750
- communications, newsletters.

TQM should not be regarded as an **extra** activity, rather as an integral part of the way business is undertaken.
To a small company these costs are **not insubstantial;** you need to judge priorities and assess how much can be completed in-house: *see section 3.*

QUALITY AND PROFIT

WILL IMPROVED QUALITY COST MORE?
MEDIUM TERM VIEW

In the medium term, as benefits arise from improved working practices, further restructuring may take place. This will give rise to reorganisation costs: 'rightsizing' is the current term. Such costs should have a quick payback.

Avoid quality becoming a convenient cost centre against which all kinds of expenditure get charged. Normal commercial criteria should apply.

QUALITY AND PROFIT

GENERIC PERFORMANCE

If we find a simple way of categorising performance, eg: low/medium/high, then we might expect that both profitability and quality improve together. The following is one such example.

A one year international study(*) by Ernst and Young Consultants covering 500 businesses in Canada, USA, Germany and Japan demonstrated:

PERFORMANCE	PROFITABILITY — RETURN ON ASSETS	PROFITABILITY — VALUE ADDED per EMPLOYEE	QUALITY — CUSTOMER SATISFACTION INDEX
LOW	< 2 %	< $47,000	LOW
MEDIUM	2 - 7 %	$47,000 - $74,000	MEDIUM
HIGH	> 7 %	> $74,000	HIGH

* Part of a 3 year study. The International Quality Study (IQS) is a comprehensive database identifying some 100 + management practices and how they relate to Quality. Trend data covers 3 years of history plus forecasts. Ref: 'Beyond Blind Faith' Dr H J Harrington, European Quality Journal June 1993

MEASURE RELATIVE PERFORMANCE

A company will benefit from Quality improvements if a <u>relative</u> difference is apparent when compared to competitors. Marketing strategies can then benefit from flexibility with pricing, value and the opportunity to grow market share - leading to improved financial performance.

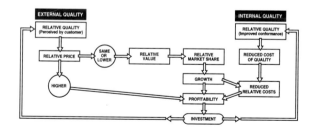

Based upon The PIMS Principles, R D Buzzell & B T Gale, The Free Press, 1987

HIGHER RATES OF RETURN

As you increase the difference in quality over your competition, so your return on
sales and investment improves.   Factors are: - customer loyalty
- repeat purchases
- avoiding price wars
- protecting share
- lower marketing costs
- growth

Source: PIMS, Linking Strategy to Performance, R D Buzzell & B T Gale

THE PRICE PERFORMANCE GRAPH

The value of your product/service can be assessed from the price performance graph.

- Positions above the line represent poor value.
- Aim to offer your customers greater value.

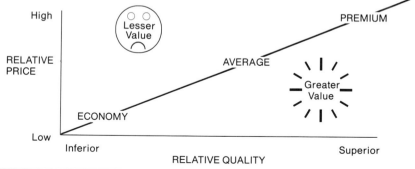

BALANCING OPERATIONAL AND STRATEGIC EFFECTIVENESS

Operational **Effectiveness**

— doing things well

Doing the wrong things right	Doing the right things right
Doing the wrong things wrong!	Doing the right things wrong

Aim to be in the top right hand box.

A lot of energy and money is wasted in the other three!

Strategic/Leadership Effectiveness
— identifying the right things **(values)**

(27)

QUALITY AND PROFIT

PRODUCTIVITY, COSTS AND QUALITY

Too often organisations regard productivity improvement, cost reduction and quality as separate problems. In fact they are often interrelated. TQM can help integrate these factors and address the root cause(s).

 PRODUCTIVITY

Example:
Reducing your workforce may increase output per head but result in overtime, increased costs and reduced quality (through higher customer complaints).

 COSTS

Example:
A company needing to cut its overall budget by 5% may apply the reduction across all cost-centres, in an attempt to be fair. But this may also result in a decline in both productivity and quality. 5% less may be required as an average but some cost centres may need to spend rather more and others even less. Priorities should be allocated.

↑ PRODUCTIVITY
↓ COSTS ↑ QUALITY

Always aim to satisfy all three.

QUALITY AND PROFIT

KEY QUESTIONS

For those just starting

- What measures do you currently have for productivity, profitability and quality; and how do you compare to competitors?
- How do your costs, prices, market share figures compare with the rest of the industry?
- Where might customer value be enhanced, and how can this be achieved without added cost?

For those who already have a TQM initiative

As above plus:

- How well have you met forecasts, and have you changed your position in the market relative to competition?
- Where are you differentiated? Is it a position that can be sustained, and is it likely to be attractive (growth, market share, profitability, customer loyalty, etc)?
- What potential remains to reduce non value-added activity and improve operational effectiveness?
- Where might strategic and leadership values be further enhanced?

NOTES

IMPLEMENTATION

IMPLEMENTATION

The so called Quality Gurus all have their own preferred approach, and their many ardent supporters. Whilst it is possible to outline some guidelines and general DO's/DONT's this book encourages an approach to TQM which is individually tailored, internally led and driven by business needs. To some degree therefore you can dip into, and adapt where appropriate from the works of Deming, Juran, Crosby etc, *(see section 8).*

A major mistake by many is to launch into TQM without proper preparation and tailoring to the organisation's needs. This section starts with a list of DO's under three headings:

- **PREPARATION / PLANNING**
- **GETTING STARTED**
- **CHANGING THE WAY WE DO BUSINESS**

and finishes with a checklist of common mistakes under **DONT's.**

PREPARATION/PLANNING
BUSINESS PLAN

DO:

✓ Start with an updated business plan — not just financial plans.

✓ Review whether the plan addresses quality related issues.

✓ Clarify current or starting position (with surveys if need be):
  - customers — what do they think of us?
  - suppliers — how easy are we to do business with?
  - employees — what is it like to work here?

IMPLEMENTATION

PREPARATION/PLANNING
SWOT ANALYSIS

DO:

✓ Check what we are good at, which strengths/capabilities should be built on.

✓ Identify improvement areas:
eg: waste, rework, absence, system faults.

✓ Review potential barriers to change:
eg: piece-work payment systems, make for stock policies, departmental politics.

PREPARATION/PLANNING
BOARD AGREEMENT

DO:

✓ Ensure that there is full board agreement and consensus on:

- sense of mission — what is the real purpose of this business?
  values   → do individuals share organisational values?
  behaviours   — are we clear which competences we wish to encourage, and do we practise what we preach?

- what the organisation has to do to achieve its mission — these goals are usually called critical success factors,
  eg: make a profit, be regarded as world class, achieve high customer satisfaction ratings

- things that matter most — these typically cut across functional boundaries and are referred to as business processes, eg: develop new products, invoice for completed work, recruit and develop people

- priorities for the organisation — which processes are most critical and which are we least competent at.

(35)

IMPLEMENTATION

PREPARATION/PLANNING
REVIEW

DO:

✓ Consider how TQM might assist your organisation in achieving these priorities and hence the business plan.

✓ Identify

- how resources should be allocated
- who should have responsibility for what
- the information systems required to track performance.

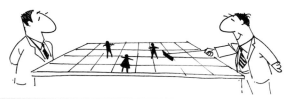

GETTING STARTED
FIRST STEPS

DO:

✓ Ensure that you have a clear way of communicating what TQM means to each of your stakeholders — shareholders, customers, suppliers and employees.

✓ Select a **manageable** number of Quality Improvement Projects (QIP's), ideally covering high, medium and low priority. The benefit of the latter is that they should be relatively easy to accomplish (eg: improving the way you answer the phone) and you can demonstrate some early benefits. High priority projects typically take longer and have greater risk associated with them.

It is important to achieve some early successes whilst still tackling those issues that are important.

IMPLEMENTATION

GETTING STARTED
STAFF TRAINING

DO:

✓ Think carefully about how to train staff and tackle these QIPs:
- Some companies start on a **top down basis**
  - in big organisations this can take a long time for the benefits to impact on staff generally.

- Others do the reverse and start **bottom up**
  - this can have the drawback of not involving senior management enough. As with quality circles interest may wane and the initiative becomes another 'flavour of the month'.

- Try taking a **diagonal slice** - this has the effect of involving people at all levels, a bit like lighting fires around the place
  - can be particularly effective when team leaders are selected for their experience and hidden talents, rather than seniority.
    Train the team leaders first in TQM concepts, problem solving skills and teamwork. Let the leaders select their teams, preferably inter-departmental and again at different levels of seniority.

GETTING STARTED
REPORT TO MANAGEMENT

DO:

✓ Demonstrate the benefits of the
QIP's to senior management.
If you form a Steering Group do
involve at least some of the board
who originally identified the
priorities. Teams should not waste
time by producing hefty reports,
but make a simple presentation
covering:

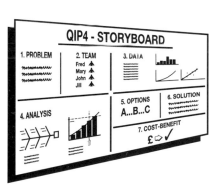

- the stages in which the project
  was tackled
- key findings
- cost-benefits
- recommendations
  — often in a visual form (called a **STORYBOARD**) using graphs/charts,
  etc, from the analysis.

(39)

GETTING STARTED
INTERNAL MARKETING

DO:

✓ Start internal marketing of TQM.

Try to avoid hype, posters and silly competitions. Whilst fun is great, it is important that the initiative is not devalued and also that expectations are not raised to a level which cannot be satisfied.
Quality Newsletters or regular articles in in-house magazines work very well; as do occasional conferences, etc.

Senior management must again play an active role, demonstrate commitment and not promise what cannot be delivered.

GETTING STARTED

CO-ORDINATION

DO:

✓ Consider the best way **(for your company)** of co-ordinating the TQM initiative. A Steering Committee may be sufficient, but most companies choose to have either a full time Quality Manager or a Co-ordinator/Facilitator, usually part time in conjunction with another role.
In either case the person should be sufficiently senior to command respect and demonstrate that TQM is to be taken seriously.

Quality Manager	FOR	- full time, dedicated, incentive to succeed
	AGAINST	- nobody else assumes any responsibility for TQM
		- if also managing an existing Quality Control or Assurance function can cause conflict.
Facilitator	FOR	- achieves results through others
		- encourages others to bear responsibility
	AGAINST	- time management, especially when priorities change, or difficulties arise
		- may be politically easy to opt out.

(41)

IMPLEMENTATION

GETTING STARTED
CUSTOMER-SUPPLIER CHAINS

DO:

✓ Encourage departments and key personnel to identify their customer-supplier chains.

This is a key philosophy to TQM. Everyone should be able to identify where they are in the chain — also who they have to agree requirements with. In some cases it can be very helpful to formalise the service with a **customer service agreement.**

If there are no customers and/or suppliers for a particular work activity, ask 'Why is this activity taking place?' ...... if there is no added-value then the task is wasteful and should probably be eliminated.
This approach is the start of **process analysis,** rigorously identifying inputs and outputs, mapping processes to improve workflow and response times.

Remember everyone has customers, internal as well as external.

GETTING STARTED
EFFECTIVE PERFORMANCE

DO:

✓ Try to break down functional barriers. Using the customer-supplier chain and process analysis techniques, multi-disciplinary teams can **often work more effectively;** or at least avoid the old 'them & us' attitude between competing functions. Departments have to learn to collaborate.

✓ Ensure that appropriate measurement systems are available to track performance and reward desired behaviours *(see section 5)*.

CHANGING THE WAY WE DO BUSINESS
SYSTEMS AND PRACTICE

DO :

✓   Endeavour to make TQM behaviours the **normal** way of working.

✓   Improve systems where it makes sense. If used properly BS 5750/ISO 9000 is fully compatible with continuous improvement. The procedures should **NOT** inhibit innovation and improvements being made wherever possible.

✓   Be prepared to share ideas and learn best practice from other companies. One of the good things about TQM is that companies are prepared to open their doors and discuss experiences. There used to be too much unnecessary secrecy (allowing for matters of commercial confidentiality). In this way companies can learn much more from 'doing' and trying new ideas.

✓   Build upon the above point by benchmarking key practices *(see section 4)*. Companies (even within the same industry) sometimes form **'clubs'** to assist with this process.

CHANGING THE WAY WE DO BUSINESS
CUSTOMERS & SUPPLIERS

DO:

✓ Be prepared to 're-engineer' the organisation so that departmental barriers do not get in the way of key processes. If organisations say that they are customer-driven then this needs to be reflected in the way that work is organised. In this way companies can achieve '**quantum leaps rather than only incremental improvements**' from their TQM initiative.

✓ Start taking key suppliers into your commercial confidence. Introduce them to TQM, share training and/or workshops. Try to work with suppliers in a **win-win** manner, it will save a lot of wasted time and often money in the long run.

✓ Start working with customers in jointly designing/specifying new systems, products, services, etc.

CHANGING THE WAY WE DO BUSINESS
ATTITUDE

DO:

✓ Engender a world class attitude in the way the company operates, not to be the best at everything — but to try to be the best at some key part of the operation.

✓ Be patient. It takes time — usually a long time — to change a company's culture.

WHAT NOT TO DO

DON'T:

✖ Do TQM just because everyone else is doing it

✖ Do TQM because your boss has been to a conference, thinks TQM is the best thing since sliced bread, and tells you to do it (and let him/her know in three months how you are getting on).

✖ Introduce too many QIP's.

✖ Try to train everybody straight away — do it just in time (JIT).

✖ Guess what the cost of quality is.
Stick to facts and do not try to incorporate non quality related costs into the equation. It will only backfire when someone looks for the subsequent savings!

WHAT NOT TO DO

DON'T:

✖ Allow consultants to take ownership. Use their skills as facilitators to the process or change agents. TQM must be driven internally and led visibly by senior executives.

✖ Let Quality systems or your passion for TQM get too far out of balance. Tom Peters once said '... the trouble is, companies either have lots of passion but no systems, or too many systems and no passion (for quality)'.

✖ Try to run before you can walk, eg: benchmarking without proper internal analysis and comparators.

✖ Give up when you first hit problems, or show signs of a plateau in performance. Concerted effort and tenacity are required over a long period of time.

WHO CAN WE ~~COPY~~ LEARN FROM?

49

BENCHMARKING

DEFINITION

Benchmarking simply means setting a point of reference or comparison.

Or in the rather more aggressive context in which the term is currently deployed:

> **'....... the search for industry best practices that lead to superior performance'**
>
> **Robert Camp**

WHO CAN WE ~~COPY~~ LEARN FROM?

BENCHMARKING

DRIVING FORCES

Why has this easy to say, hard to do, platitude become so popular? Apart from the pressure to do things faster (Time-Based competition) there are at least three **key driving forces:**

(1) **global competition:** new competitors are likely to emerge from outside your home market.

(2) **Quality Awards** actively encourage business to compete and defend markets internationally — these awards require **self assessment** of which benchmarking processes are a key component.

(3) After small incremental improvements/evolutionary changes run out, TQM initiatives need a **breakthrough** to achieve higher and continuous levels of improvement. If competition is improving at a faster rate the only way to improve your relative quality is a 'quantum leap' or breakthrough **that will enable you to leapfrog (rather than catch up)** the opposition.

WHO CAN WE ~~COPY~~ LEARN FROM?

BENCHMARKING
WHY DO IT?

The big change for many is simply to start looking **outwards.** Companies often get so absorbed with their own improvement initiatives that they forget to keep an eye on what others are up to. But benchmarking is often at its most successful when it reviews best practice from completely different industries.

Which is your company?

- external perspective ● market driven ● proactive
- innovative ● fully conversant with customer requirements, etc?

OR

- inward looking ● reactive ● not customer orientated
- experts at 'not invented here', and ● 'if it ain't bust don't fix it'?

Even the most sophisticated and advanced organisations are striving to get better at being better — and benchmarking helps.

WHO CAN WE ~~COPY~~ LEARN FROM?

BENCHMARKING

WHAT IS INVOLVED? (1)

Companies develop their own detailed approach to benchmarking, but typically the key steps are:

STEP 1:   Decide **what process** to benchmark.

Before zooming off to visit the world's best in Japan or the USA (or wherever) considerable **planning** is required.

You must know:
- what to look for
- what questions to ask
- how to interpret results.

Bear in mind, with any relationship you establish, that you will need to be able to reciprocate.

One way of selecting suitable processes is to review the cost chain, looking for areas of business leverage and significant improvement potential.

Examples could include material procurement, product manufacture or sourcing, warehousing and distribution.

BENCHMARKING

WHAT IS INVOLVED? (2)

STEP 2:   Collect data and **understand your own internal process.**

Usually done by mapping the process (breaking into small elements and identifying the flows of information, materials, product, etc).

For key elements:
- review inputs and outputs, eg: which ones add value?
- is it the way the customer wants it?
- identify the results of the process
- identify key performance measures that are then applicable.

Having done this analysis thoroughly you are in a position to find out how others undertake a similar process. (Remember the typical childhood dilemma of '... show me yours, and I'll show you mine' which is usually unfair on whoever goes first!) In the US there is a code of practice for the exchange of information; think through any legal or commercial issues.

BENCHMARKING

WHAT IS INVOLVED? (3)

STEP 3: Identify **who is the best in class?**

Sources of information are: consultancies, business schools, trade associations, business libraries, databases, journals, TV/Radio. Some companies form clubs to exchange information, eg: on pay and conditions. Don't be too narrow in approach; some of the best gains have come from outside your own industry:

- an ammunitions manufacturer improved the finish on its shell cases from benchmarking a cosmetics lipstick producer

- a hospital theatre compared its scheduling with a high performing airline timetable process

- a computer distributor learned from a major high street retailer about inventory management and logistics

- a high tech, high product quality company learned from a financial services. organisation about how to improve customer service.

In the US a Benchmarking Clearing House was set up in Houston in 1991; a similar organisation was established in the UK in Hemel Hempstead during 1993.

(55)

BENCHMARKING

WHAT IS INVOLVED? (4)

STEP 4: Adapt and improve.

Now analyse your own performance to see how it can be improved.

Look

Improve → Copy

Adapt

This is really the stage of **making it happen,** getting people involved. The board might well seek benchmarking evidence that a capital investment proposal is based on what can be achieved.
Anti Not Invented Here pills may also be useful!

In ATT&T they have 12 steps to their process, IBM have 16 and Xerox 10. Always tailor, and make your approach company specific.

TYPES OF PARTNER

Benchmarking partners are usually classified under four headings. As you gain experience and confidence it may be appropriate to undertake a number of different projects with various groups of partners.

1. Internal   Compares departments, sites, countries, etc, for the same company.
A good place to start benchmarking!
Very relevant, easy to get information but inward looking.

2. Competitive   Compares performance with direct competitors.
Very relevant, may be difficult to get data (but often easier than at first thought), may only catch up, not overtake.

3. Functional   Compares with the best in similar fields or activities. Requires high discipline, easier to collect data, high innovation.

4. Generic   Compares with the best from all industry groupings. More complex, requires high resource but huge gains possible!

WHO CAN WE ~~COPY~~ LEARN FROM?

PUTTING IN CONTEXT

TRUTHS

For benchmarking to succeed the following should be regarded as
MUSTS :

senior management support   - commitment, understanding and participation

understanding own process   - a prerequisite to finding out more from others

teamwork   - involve those who know the work, and gain their enthusiasm in making improvements

planning   - needs to be organised, championed and goals set

part of strategy   - identify critical success factors and overall impact

PUTTING IN CONTEXT

UNTRUTHS

However, be aware of the following **myths which are untrue:**

Benchmarking is:

just competitor analysis	- no, you look at specific processes, and the partners may not be competitors
copying	- why reinvent the wheel? Usually undertaken to improve; it is rarely appropriate to copy anyway
just numbers	- the key is the **way** it is done. You then need the right measures
only applicable to manufacturing	- applies to all sectors
competitors won't share	- don't expect them to share everything, but that still leaves a lot that can help to grow the industry as a whole

See further: 'Taking on the World', C. Jackson Grayson Jnr, TQM Magazine June 1992

WHO CAN WE ~~COPY~~ LEARN FROM?

SIZE OF BUSINESS

- You do not have to be big

- Small businesses can still benefit from benchmarking

- **LOOK** — what are 'they' doing that's different?

  LEARN — where can 'we' learn from them?

  LISTEN — to 'our' experts; how can we adapt and
  improve our processes?

PERFORMANCE MEASUREMENT

MANAGEMENT OF PERFORMANCE

Performance measurement is crucial in the success of a Quality initiative. If you do not measure (correctly) the improvements you are seeking then no amount of passion, or number of improvement teams, will be sufficient.

A number of companies are also introducing rather more formal methods of **performance management,** eg:

- linking of corporate goals with department/individual targets
- identifying the key result areas
- identifying critical success factors
- clarifying key competences.

These are in addition to performance appraisal and objective setting. Performance measurement is important, both for business success and the continuous improvement goal.

WHAT YOU MEASURE ...

WYMIWYG

W hat
Y ou
M easure
I s
W hat
Y ou
G et

1 It the improvement is not taken sufficiently seriously to be measured – then it is unlikely to be achieved or sustained.

2 What gets measured often determines how people behave.

PERFORMANCE MEASUREMENT

TYPES OF MEASURE

Traditionally, too much reliance has been placed on analysis of management accounts data against set standards, without also assessing added value and effective use of resources.

Traditional performance measures emphasised 'how' work was undertaken:

● analyse the work elements, design an effective sequence, ensure that everyone follows that precise method. Hence, industrial engineering techniques such as: work study, organisation & methods, payment by results, etc.

Continuous improvement shifts emphasis from method to results and harnesses people's creativity and innovation:

● real, sustained performance improvement comes from competent motivated people who will find their own best way of working. Thus the so called scientific approach has often been replaced with: assessment centres, widespread training in the use of brainstorming, problem solving and simple statistical analysis.

INFLUENCES ON PERFORMANCE

There are many factors which influence performance, some will be within your
control but others outside your control:

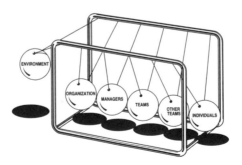

PERFORMANCE MEASUREMENT

BALANCED SCORECARD

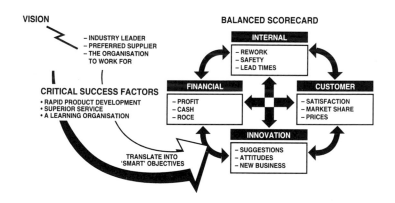

66

BALANCED SCORECARD

This approach provides a way of translating strategic objectives into those performance measures which are really critical. The scorecard is 'balanced' because it takes account of the tradeoffs between competing dynamics such as internal/external/financial/customer, etc, etc.

1. Vision of where the organisation should be going.
2. Critical success factors if the vision is to be achieved.
3. How the company would then differ:

      to shareholders .... Financial Perspective
      to customers .... Customer Perspective
      internal processes .... Internal Perspective
      ability to grow .... Innovation and Learning

IDENTIFYING PERFORMANCE MEASURES

Many companies have ways of measuring their strategic/competitive performance and also the quality of their product and/or service. But few measure employee and customer satisfaction.

The trick is to replace 'either/or' thinking with Performance Indicators that are both:

- financial **and** non-financial
- tangible **and** intangible
- internal **and** external
- top down **and** bottom up

PERFORMANCE INDICATOR	PERFORMANCE MEASURE
Employee related	Employee satisfaction, attendance, turnover, safety, suggestions, etc
Operational	Reliability, delivery, processing times, lead times, inventory turnover, errors, costs of rework, etc
Customer Satisfaction	Overall index, retention and complaints
Market and Financial	Market share, cash, profit, ROA, ROS, sales per employee, etc

PERFORMANCE MEASUREMENT

SMART OBJECTIVES

In setting objectives, remember that the focus should be on:

results **NOT** activities   ends **NOT** means   output **NOT** input

- The most important areas for a person, job or process may be referred to as **Key Result Areas** (These are the desired outputs).
- The metric (subject to continuous improvement) by which performance is judged acceptable is the **Standard.**
- The target or objective should be stretching and in excess of the standard, whenever practical and conform to **SMART criteria:**

  S pecific
  M easurable
  A chievable
  R esults orientated
  T ime bound

PERFORMANCE MEASUREMENT

SMART OBJECTIVES
EXAMPLE

For example, for an operations manager:

Key result area	Output level
Performance indicator	Output per week per product
Objective	To increase output of product x by 5% in the next 9 months

Attention should be paid to careful wording.
Avoid managerial weasel words such as maximum, optimise, justifiable, etc, which indicate direction but do not define how far.

PERFORMANCE MEASUREMENT

SELF ASSESSMENT

... or how to carry out your own company HEALTH CHECK!

Measuring the **financial** health of a business is well documented, if not always well understood.

—Measuring the **Strategic and Quality** 'health' of a business is not straightforward; hence the growing popularity of self-assessment frameworks.

—Some companies use these 'models' to compete for major Quality Awards, eg:

- Deming (Japan)
- European Foundation for Quality Management
- Baldrige (USA)

- British Quality Foundation (UK - new 1994)
- Hong Kong Management Association

External assessors judge the submissions against a range of criteria.

Many companies use these frameworks for continuous improvement without any desire to enter a competition.

PERFORMANCE MEASUREMENT

QUALITY FRAMEWORKS (1)

USA Quality Award

In the Baldrige framework, points are allocated and weighted as follows:

Customer satisfaction 30%

Leadership 10%

Quality results 18%

Information and Analysis 7%

Human Resource utilisation 15%

Strategic Quality Planning 6%

Quality Assurance systems 14%

QUALITY FRAMEWORKS (2)

European Model for TQM

This European framework shows the linkages and comparative weightings between the components. For your own self assessment different weightings might be appropriate.

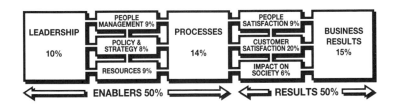

QUALITY FRAMEWORKS (3)

Hong Kong Quality Award framework

Here is a third framework, this time from the Hong Kong Management Association. The point as always is to find a way of assessing your own performance in ways other than purely financial.

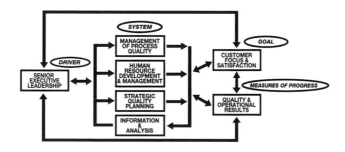

PERFORMANCE REVIEW

TQM has helped encourage a number of changes with regard to appraisal/performance review systems.

Customer focus
- The customer is the true judge of performance.

- Within the appraisal assessment is based on the views of key internal and/or external customers.

- The boss can then focus more on linking company/department/individual targets and agreeing those areas where resources or other help may be required.

Reward
- It is important to place the emphasis on recognition of effort and achievement. This becomes part of the desired culture change for TQM.

- Financial incentives or bonus payments, especially at an individual level, can be divisive and counter to effective teamwork and TQM.

PERFORMANCE REVIEW

Career
- With a trend towards flatter structures fewer opportunities are available, particularly at middle management level. Career development happens increasingly through sideways moves, involvement in multi functional project teams and so on.

Competences
- As well as government schemes like MCI and NVQ, many organisations are identifying skills and behaviours appropriate to them.

- This sets **standards** for assessing an individual's capability to undertake a particular role.

- Competences are then linked to performance indicators, and often to specified company values and behaviours, eg: 'management by wandering around', 'treat company assets as your own'.

- Competences can become a form of 'company language'. This aids the Quality process by **reinforcing desirable behaviours** and placing emphasis on fact rather than personality.

QUALITY SYSTEMS

QUALITY SYSTEMS

ISO 9000
WHAT IS IT?

- An international standard for quality assurance best known, in the UK, as **BS 5750**.
- Launched in 1979.
- Approx 20,000 firms in Britain registered.

Some experts have argued that BS 5750 provides a good basis or platform from which to launch TQM.

Points in favour:
- provides some discipline through procedures
- reduces variation.

Points against:
- can become a bureaucratic nightmare, outweighing the benefits
- is increasingly used to pressure suppliers.

Much depends on the industry norms, eg: in petrochemicals, high levels of safety demand assurance levels in excess of BS 5750.

QUALITY SYSTEMS

ISO 9000
KEY ISSUES

- Is ISO 9000 essential to compete in our industry?

- Would it aid marketing or company image?

- Would procedures reduce innovation and creativity (can usually be avoided if not too rigid)?

- Can the organisation cope with yet another demanding project?

QUALITY SYSTEMS

ISO 9000
WHAT WOULD WE HAVE TO DO?

Approach

- To develop, refine, review and update working practices
    - what is done?
    - why is it done?
    - where is the requirement met?
    - who is responsible?
    - how is it done?

It is important **not** simply to document what is done without going through the above process. You also need to involve staff who actually do the job in writing the appropriate procedure, otherwise the auditors will catch you out!

Policy

- A statement of the company policy on quality prefaces a procedures manual, documenting how key activities or processes are undertaken.

QUALITY SYSTEMS

ISO 9000
HOW LONG?

Timescale

- Typical phases in developing a manual and gaining accreditation are:

  1. terms of reference, objectives, timetable
  2. interim report and action plan
  3. full report and draft quality manual
  4. internal audit followed by external assessment.

Overall usually 1 year and more

Challenge

- Does the company have capable resources and processes?

  Are appropriate procedures and systems available?

IT IS USUALLY ADVISABLE TO SEEK THE HELP OF A SPECIALIST CONSULTANT WHO IS PERSONALLY RECOMMENDED.

QUALITY SYSTEMS

PROBLEM SOLVING PROCESS

This is a systematic way of tackling problems, and endeavouring to find the **root cause** (so that good old problem No.185 doesn't keep coming back to haunt you!).

The most simple is known as the PLAN-DO-CHECK-ACT cycle. It is intended to act as a check that in solving problems you do not jump to solutions but go through a methodical process.
Companies often take these 4 stages and break them down into further elements relevant to their own environment.

Eg: 1. state problem
2. select team
3. take ownership
4. analyse data
5. identify potential solutions
6. develop action plan for chosen solution
7. present and sell solution
8. implement plan
9. monitor and evaluate

PLAN

ACT → → DO

↖ ↙
CHECK

QUALITY SYSTEMS

DEPARTMENTAL PROCESS ANALYSIS (DPA)

Systematically reviewing what a department (or function) actually does, why, and seeking ways of improving key processes is known as DPA.

This technique or approach can be helpful in a number of ways, to:

- enable a team or department to apply TQM to their own environment
- review practices, eliminate waste, etc; may be particularly helpful following a reorganisation or staff changes
- improve relationships with other functions or teams, especially where close co-operation is required
- identify clearly the internal customer and supplier linkages
- pave the way for more radical reorganisation where traditional functional boundaries are redefined. This approach essentially reverse engineers the external customer needs back through the organisation — known as Business Process Re-engineering (BPR).

QUALITY SYSTEMS

DEPARTMENTAL PROCESS ANALYSIS (DPA)
EXAMPLE

Suppose, for example, a Personnel department wished to review the processes for recruiting staff, dealing with resignations or the use made of routine reports, etc. Then **DPA seeks answers to the following questions:**

1. What is the real purpose of the department, and what service do we offer?
2. Has the nature of the service required now altered? Does our boss agree?
3. How do our internal customers want things to be done?
4. Why are we doing this, is there another better way?
5. Does our work satisfy any external customer needs?
6. Do our suppliers understand our needs, timescales, resource constraints, etc?

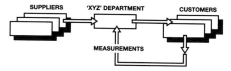

Is there conformance to requirements?

QUALITY SYSTEMS

SERVICE LEVELS

Having determined which parts of the process(es) add value, you may need to agree service levels both tangible and intangible, for example:

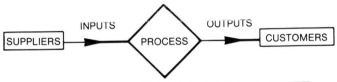

TANGIBLE	INTANGIBLE
Quantity	Style
Reliability	Attitude to change
On-time delivery	Timing
Quality	Clarity
Format	Willingness to help

SERVICE LEVELS
COMPARISONS

Then make comparisons (perhaps using benchmarking techniques *see chapter 4*) with how other similar functions/departments/processes, etc, are organised, eg:

— do they achieve higher customer satisfaction levels?
— how much higher?
— why are they higher?
— what lessons can be learnt from them?
— how can performance be further improved?

TQM IN EUROPE

EUROPEAN EXPERIENCES

In Europe lots of TQM programmes have failed. In particular, US led consultancy/training packages have been unsuccessful, underscoring the need for Europe to follow a different route from what may have worked in Japan or USA.

Recent research * by Ashridge into European experience has shown that **TQM can and does work** when taken seriously by companies intent on introducing key processes consistent with TQM principles.

DO	DON'T
• Involve people throughout the organisation. • Encourage people to learn through their actions — including mistakes. • Foster collaboration across business units and between functions. • Push people to tackle the root causes of problems. • Maintain an external customer focus.	• Impose TQM from the top. • Encourage people to go through the motions of TQM. • Incite unhealthy levels of competition between departments. • Allow solutions which only address the symptoms. • Become preoccupied with internal issues.

* Making Quality Work — Lessons from Europe's leading companies, published by the Economist Intelligence Unit, London, 1992. The Ashridge team led by George Binney looked at some 50 organisations in total, and 6 in detail— all having five or more years' experience of introducing TQM processes.

LESSONS FROM EUROPE

Who needs TQM?

It is increasingly ignored at your peril.

FAILS when	● incremental changes only
	● driven by internal needs
	● training is company wide
SUCCEEDS when	● challenges from benchmarking world class performance
	● European Foundation for Quality Management (**EFQM)** criteria or similar are used for measuring performance improvement
	● principles are defined in terms of continuous improvement and value to the customer
	● relative quality advantages lead to increased financial returns
	● training is focused.

89

LESSONS FROM EUROPE

What do they mean by TQM?

- Broad organisational and cultural change.
- Continuous improvement through the process of delighting customers.
- Creating an environment where people bring the same energy and ability as they deploy outside.

How do you implement?

- Easy to say but hard to do!
- Radical rethinking by management and a shift of power away from shareholders towards customers, suppliers and employees.
- Forthright, listening style of leadership.
- Provoke change where necessary, rather than impose it — mirror the principles of empowerment.
- Learn through doing and train 'just-in-time'.

CHECKLISTS

QUALITY OR FINANCIALLY ORIENTATED?

This questionnaire reviews how well quality is ingrained in different parts of the business. It can be helpful to compare different interpretations and the underlying reasons.

Part 2 explores the same issues from a financial perspective. This can help to reveal where the real priorities are in the business and a little about the style and leadership. For example, in a strongly financial control company the measurement systems and perhaps short term focus may be in conflict with the longer term customer driven principles of quality.

TQM QUESTIONNAIRE

PART 1: QUALITY AWARENESS

Please indicate how your company or organisation currently manages quality by circling the number on the scale that most closely indicates your current behaviour or practice.

	TO A VERY LIMITED EXTENT		TO A MODERATE EXTENT		TO A VERY GREAT EXTENT
1. Quality (of service) is a key issue in our regular business reviews, meetings and business planning process (not just when problems exist).	1	2	3	4	5
2. When we recruit and select new employees at all levels, we look first and foremost for people with good service skills.	1	2	3	4	5
3. Ideas for service and quality improvement from employees are positively valued and rewarded.	1	2	3	4	5
4. All employees receive training in such a way that they understand service quality concepts and why they are important.	1	2	3	4	5

CHECKLISTS

TQM QUESTIONNAIRE
PART 1: QUALITY AWARENESS

		TO A VERY LIMITED EXTENT	TO A MODERATE EXTENT		TO A VERY GREAT EXTENT	
5.	A common definition of service quality, along with processes to ensure clear requirements for service delivery, is in use for all employees.	1	2	3	4	5
6.	Quality (of service) performance is a heavily weighted part of our staff's performance appraisals, salary increases, and/or bonuses.	1	2	3	4	5
7.	Our standards for quality improvement inspire exceptional performance rather than demanding a standard level of performance.	1	2	3	4	5
8.	Our public relations, sales, advertising and promotional messages stress our continued strong performance on quality (or what we're doing to improve it).	1	2	3	4	5
9.	If quality deteriorates, we take immediate action with top priority to identify and resolve the root cause of the problem.	1	2	3	4	5
10.	We regularly measure our quality and report it to all employees.	1	2	3	4	5

(94) Total (added circled values) _____

CHECKLISTS

TQM QUESTIONNAIRE
PART 2: FINANCIAL AWARENESS

	TO A VERY LIMITED EXTENT		TO A MODERATE EXTENT		TO A VERY GREAT EXTENT
1. Profitability is a key issue in our regular business reviews, meetings and business planning process (not just when problems exist).	1	2	3	4	5
2. When we recruit and select new employees at all levels, we look first and foremost for people with good financial skills.	1	2	3	4	5
3. Ideas for profit and cost improvement from employees are positively valued and rewarded.	1	2	3	4	5
4. All employees receive training in such a way that they understand financial concepts and why they are important.	1	2	3	4	5
5. A common definition of profit, along with processes to ensure clear requirements for financial control, is in use for all employees.	1	2	3	4	5

TQM QUESTIONNAIRE

PART 2: FINANCIAL AWARENESS

		TO A VERY LIMITED EXTENT		TO A MODERATE EXTENT		TO A VERY GREAT EXTENT
6.	Budget/Financial performance is a heavily weighted part of our staff's performance appraisals, salary increases, and/or bonuses.	1	2	3	4	5
7.	Our standards for profit improvement inspire exceptional performance rather than demanding a standard level of performance.	1	2	3	4	5
8.	Our public relations, sales, advertising and promotional messages stress our continued strong performance on cost control (or what we're doing to improve it).	1	2	3	4	5
9.	If profitability deteriorates, we take immediate action with top priority to identify and resolve the root cause of the problem.	1	2	3	4	5
10.	We regularly measure our financial performance and report it to all employees.	1	2	3	4	5

Total (added circled values) _____

QUALITY OR ORDINARY COMPANY?

This is a simple way, again using a 1 — 5 scale, for assessing perceptions of the business; and can be helpful in initial workshops or focus groups. Some of the terms used are deliberately provocative to force a debate and raise questions in people's minds. The questions can of course be amended to reflect specific company or industry issues.

WHICH IS YOUR COMPANY?

ORDINARY COMPANY	1	2	3	4	5	QUALITY COMPANY
Customer satisfaction comes after profits						Profits come from customer satisfaction
Focus on detecting problems						Focus on preventing problems
Cost containment through cutting						Cost containment through disciplined approach to own operations and to the supply chain
Values numbers						Values people
Low spending on training						High spending on training
Vague about goals/roles/standards at any levels						Explicit and disciplined about goals/roles/standards at all levels

Rate your own company on a range from 1 (very ordinary) to 5 (quality)

CHECKLISTS

QUALITY OR ORDINARY COMPANY?

ORDINARY COMPANY	1	2	3	4	5	QUALITY COMPANY
Treats complaints as a nuisance						Treats complaints as an opportunity to learn
In awe of technology						Uses technology selectively under management control
Runs by systems						Runs by people working with other people
Sees quality/productivity/cost reduction as separate endeavours						Restless search for improvement of the business with quality/ productivity/cost reduction as indivisible elements
People do not know where they fit in the Quality Chain						Manages the Quality Chain

Rate your own company on a range from 1 (very ordinary) to 5 (quality)

CHANGING THE CULTURE

When striving for new ways of working, it is important to give examples of the change in culture that you wish to achieve. Here are a few examples:

OLD CULTURE
- Quick fix
- Major breakthroughs
- Quality on the agenda
- Talk about quality
- Will this improve profit
- Not invented here
- Keep my head down
- Look for good feedback
- Put others' work right
- Spend company money
- Manage tasks

NEW CULTURE
- Right first time
- Continuous small improvements
- Quality first on the agenda
- 'Walk about' quality
- Will this improve customer service
- Not rejected here
- Show interest in helping others
- Welcome feedback both good and bad
- Make sure they know you had to put it right
- Spend it as if it were your own
- Manage people

CHECKLISTS

COST OF QUALITY

A number of companies have found it helpful to clarify costs associated with poor quality, rework, failure, etc — often as a way of reinforcing the strategic importance of quality and gaining commitment. Measuring progress in reducing the costs over time may then become one way of tracking quality improvement.

Typical categories are:

- Failure - internal
  - external (eg: supplier based)

- Appraisal - inspection
  - checking
  - testing

- Prevention - statistical process control
  - ISO 9000 accreditation

The aim is to reduce the total of these categories over time and also to reduce significantly the proportion of Failure and Appraisal costs, whilst putting more effort, where appropriate, into Prevention.

CHECKLISTS

COST OF QUALITY
DO'S AND DON'TS

Some selected lessons *(based upon 'Quality Costing', Dale & Plunkett)*

DO:
1. Clarify the purpose.
2. Corroborate data and use Accounts based data where possible.
3. Start with failure costs and apply 'pareto' (80:20) principles.
4. Target appraisal costs for reduction.
5. Publicise cost of mistakes (eg: price of scrap wrapping paper, etc).
6. Introduce a simple reporting system.

DON'T:
1. Be too ambitious, you should start small.
2. Underestimate difficulties with definitions.
3. Waste time on small cost elements.
4. Guess.
5. Be constrained by the normal categories.
6. Forget prevention will be the hardest category to cost.

CHECKLISTS

CUSTOMER – SUPPLIER SURVEY

Typical approach:

1. Plan
   - who to approach?
   - what form of survey (face to face, telephone, independent, etc)?
   - who will undertake the survey?
   - what questions should be posed?

2. Survey
   - Format to include
     - details — name/date/place
     - what are we like to work with?
     - specific products/services supplied
     - vendor rating — is there a system?
     - satisfaction index (1 — 100, etc)
     - frequency of contact
     - what would you like to see improved?
     - thank you for participation

3. Action Plan
   - what should be improved?
   - priorities?
   - resource allocation?
   - progress reporting

The planning and design of such surveys could be a team task/part of a quality improvement exercise.

GURUS – KEY APPROACHES

The number of 'experts' in this field has grown rapidly in recent years. Dr Deming and Dr Juran are widely acclaimed for taking their ideas on quality control and assurance from the US to Japan — and helping the latter achieve a radical improvement in product quality. The ideas were then taken on a company wide basis, beyond that of simply manufacturing or operations. Crosby 'popularised' many of the principles, with a series of easy to digest books and videos based on his own extensive experience and approach to training.

At the risk of gross simplification, here are some of the key points and differences in approach:

Dr W E Deming

- Focus on shop floor based (small) improvements and shared responsibility.
- Emphasis upon statistical process control and techniques.
- Radical approach — avoid incentive rewards, stop short termism, develop long term relationships with vendors, etc.
- Learn how to change, drive out fear.

GURUS – KEY APPROACHES

Dr J M Juran

- Focus on 'fitness for use' and management control.
- Emphasis upon cost of quality and identifying a few vital projects that will provide breakthroughs.
- Quality professionals take responsibility for planning and co-ordination .
- Extensive use of surveys.

Philip B Crosby

- Quality is 'free' and conformance to requirements.
- Emphasis on 'zero defects' culture.
- Measure the cost of quality.
- Management responsible for fixing the problems.
- Prevent errors.

USEFUL BITS AND PIECES

Contacts

BSI
BSI Quality Assurance
PO Box 375
Milton Keynes
MK14 6LL
Tel: 01908 220908

DTI
Department of Trade and Industry
Management and Technology Services
Room 4. 18
151 Buckingham Palace Road
London SW1W 9SS
Tel: 0171 215 8142

LLOYDS
Quality Assurance Dept
Engineering Services Group
Lloyds Register House
29 Wellesley Road
Croydon CR0 2AJ
Tel: 0181 681 4040

EFQM
European Foundation for Quality
Management
Avenue des Pleiades 19c
B1200 Bruxelles, Belgium
Tel: + 32 2 775 3511

BQF
British Quality Foundation
Vigilant House
120 Wilton Road
London SW1V 1JZ
Tel: 0171 931 0607

Best Practice Club

IFS International Ltd
Freepost BF112
Wolseley Business Park
Kempston
Bedford MK42 7BR
Tel: 01234 853605

Benchmarking

The Benchmarking Centre Ltd
Truscon House
Station Road
Gerrards Cross
Bucks SL9 8ES
Tel: 01753 890070
Fax: 01753 893070

CHECKLISTS

REFERENCES/SOURCE OF INFORMATION

Journals

- **European Quality**
  European Quality Publications Ltd
  172 Nth. Gower Street
  London NW1 2ND
  Tel: 0171 388 7362

- **International Journal of Quality & Reliability Management**
- **Managing Service Quality**
- **The TQM Magazine**

All: MCB University Press Ltd
60/62 Toller Lane
Bradford
West Yorkshire BD8 9BY
Tel: 01274 499821

Making Quality Work:
Lessons from Europe's leading companies
The Economist Intelligence Unit/
Ashridge Management Guide
Special Report No.P655, 1992

Building Total Quality:
A Guide for Management, Tito Conti
Chapman & Hall, 1993

Quality Costing, Dale & Plunkett
Chapman & Hall, 1993

The PIMS (Profit Impact of Market Strategy) Principles
Linking Strategy to Performance
Buzzell & Gale, The Free Press, Macmillan, 1987

Quality Without Tears
The Art of Hassle Free Management
Philip B Crosby, Plume Printing, 1985

About the Author

Anthony Mitchell, BSc MSc DIC CEng FIEE

Anthony is Director of the European Partnership MBA at Ashridge (an International Management and Organisation Development Centre). He is subject leader in Operations Management for the MBA degree programmes and Client Director for VNU. Anthony teaches and consults in the areas of strategy, operations, TQM and performance management.

Since joining Ashridge in 1988 he has worked throughout Europe, as well as the Middle East and Far East.

Whilst with GEC Marconi, Anthony graduated in Industrial Engineering and Management Science working in design, R&D and Operational Research. His experience broadened into Financial and Legal Services with Touche Ross Management Consultants and then Gallaher Limited where he held a number of posts in management services, production management and personnel.

He is married with two young children and runs a consultancy, Anthony Mitchell Associates.

Contact

Langdale Court, Alderpark Meadow, Long Marston, Tring, Hertfordshire, HP23 4RB
Telephone: 01296 662498   Fax: 01296 662263   E-mail: am.associates@virgin.net

Acknowledgement

To the patience of Cori, Francesca and Oliver; and help from Dave Jones and Angela Hunt with computers and manuscript.

ORDER FORM

Your details

Name _____

Position _____

Company _____

Address _____

_____

_____

Telephone _____

Facsimile _____

E-mail _____

VAT No. (EC companies) _____

Your Order Ref _____

Please send me:

No. copies

The _Quality_ _____ Pocketbook ☐

The _____ Pocketbook ☐

The _____ Pocketbook ☐

The _____ Pocketbook ☐

The _____ Pocketbook ☐

Order by Post

MANAGEMENT POCKETBOOKS LTD
14 EAST STREET ALRESFORD HAMPSHIRE SO24 9EE UK

Order by Phone, Fax or Internet

Telephone: +44 (0)1962 735573
Facsimile: +44 (0)1962 733637
E-mail: pocketbks@aol.com
http://members.aol.com/pocketbks

Customers in USA should contact:
Stylus Publishing, LLC, 22883 Quicksilver Drive,
Sterling, VA 20166-2012 Telephone: 703 661 1500
Facsimile: 703 661 1501 E-mail: styluspub@aol.com